In memory of John Townsend

Jonny Trunk

wrappers delight

FUEL

FOREWORD
Jarvis Cocker

This book will give you toothache.

Before we get on to aspects of design, let's just take a little time to think about what these wrappers actually contained. A generation of children raised on bubble gum, fizzy drinks and sweet cigarettes – in the days before sugar tax, when E numbers were a signifier of quality and sophistication. It's a wonder any of us who lived through this era have any teeth left at all.

This book will give you a headache.

All these products were aimed at kids – but they gave a peculiar foretaste of the adult world we could expect to grow up into. It would seem the main thing we were be expected to do as adults was smoke – the afore-mentioned sweet cigarettes, coconut tobacco (my personal favourite, see page 54), liquorice pipes and grotesque chocolate cigars (page 164).

Career options were law enforcer, space explorer, racing driver, footballer or pop star. Failing that, you could always become a monster. No wonder we just couldn't wait to grow up.

This book will make you misty-eyed.

If you're of a certain age these wrappers will speak to you deeply of your desires as a child. The one that presses my buttons is the image of the mini racing-car construction kits on page 24. This product is unusual in that it didn't even pretend to be a sweet – unlike most of the tattoos and trading cards featured here, which also contained a sliver of brittle, bright pink gum that could draw blood if not chewed carefully. These kits were unapologetic tat. I vividly remember working out how to get money out of my ceramic piggy-bank by jamming a knife blade in the slot and then holding it upside down and shaking it. As soon as I had liberated enough coins I went to the corner shop and bought one of these. Then I ran home to construct it – which took about two minutes. So I jammed the knife into the slot again to get more cash and rushed off to the shop again to buy another one. This went on all day. I was like a nine-year-old crack addict. The world of addiction abruptly reared its ugly head in the suburbs of Sheffield.

Lucky bags are the other item to provoke an almost Pavlovian response in me: what's lucky about a bag containing the sweepings from a novelty factory floor with a couple of sweets thrown in? But it was the MYSTERY that had us hooked – what if something really, really precious was in there?

It never was, of course – no matter how many times we tried. So in that sense the wrappers featured in this book were the perfect preparation for life in a late-capitalist consumer society: the package promised so much but never delivered on that promise. They were simply designed to separate kids from their loose change as effectively as possible. They were like those mythical beads supposedly used to buy Manhattan Island from the Native Americans.

This book will give you closure.

This is by far the safest way to consume these products. To see them for what they really were. To focus on what was important about them all along: the designs that hooked in an entire generation, the pretty pictures that spoke to our primal desires. At this distance, preserved for all time upon these pages, they are beautiful.

Go on…

Feast your eyes.

INTRODUCTION
Jonny Trunk

It all began with an email from a Mr Rick Weedon in December 2016. It contained a link to a musical mix he'd made using old advertising flexi discs.

Now, anyone who knows me or Trunk Records (my record company) will recognise that this would excite me in many ways. I looked online. I listened. The mix was fascinating, mainly because I'd never come across most of the flexi discs featured – and I thought I knew that scene pretty well. So I contacted Rick and asked him where he got them from. He told me they belonged to John Townsend, the father of his friend Robin. John had passed away recently and his old house was full of boxes of all sorts of things, including the flexi discs.

John Townsend had been a big collector of ephemera – and now Robin, with his wife Paula, had started the huge task of sifting through the collection and selling some of it. So I asked for Robin's number to see if I could buy the discs.

Pretty much the next day I was sitting with Robin in his father's house in Stockport, drinking coffee and listening to BBC Radio 2's *PopMaster*. I'd driven up from London to take a look at the records – which I bought – and to see the rest of his father's collection.

Nothing quite prepared me for what I found. The five-bedroom house was full of boxes, with boxes on top of boxes, and more on top of those. And there were bags everywhere. And all the shelves were full. And there were some rooms you couldn't get into. And the attic was full. And the summerhouse outside was full. And the caravan outside was full too. And on every inch of everywhere there was something.

Once I'd explained to him that I could maybe make things with his father's ephemera before he sold it – a book or some art or some T-shirts – and so bring in a bit of money for him at the same time, Robin was up for letting me have a look around. I'd always wanted to do a book with crisp packets in it and Robin said his father had a crisp packet file somewhere.

My first dig around with Robin was strangely intense. There was so much stuff and looking through even a single box would lead to a sit down and another cuppa. Each box could well be full of files, envelopes, plastic bags or more boxes, all containing another micro collection of things, or things that were part of another collection, or things that seemed just random. These were all small items – cards, tickets, packets, badges, pamphlets, labels, leaflets. Or there would be a small box with three mini collections inside it of labelled cards from football or outer space or the local petrol station, each secured with a rubber band.

There were also 1970s ice-cream tubs full of unfiled papers and packets. There were bin bags, boxes and more files. There were chests of drawers full of stuff too – and the odd suitcase. At times it felt as if the intensity and focus required to collect such an extraordinary amount of material were being released to rub off on us as we dug around.

John Townsend was no ordinary collector. Having spent a full day looking through his stuff, I came to the conclusion that his collection of printed silk items was world class. His collection of tobacco and cigarette flags and silks was world class too. His collections of soap-related advertising, of first-day covers, of Port Sunlight postcards, of early cigarette cards and even of playing cards were all world class. But I wasn't interested in any of that. For me, it was all about the sweets. Well, mostly about the sweets…

Behind a series of boxes and running into a tall, thin chest of drawers was a set of blue folders. These were all labelled with Dymo tape and were arranged in alphabetical order. Filed by brand was a collection of sweet-related wrappers. But not the usual Mars, Marathon or Milky Way packets – no, these were far more obscure. And far more exciting. There were companies I'd never heard of, chews I'd not seen for four decades – Dad's Army sweet cigarettes, Punk gum, Lolly Gobble Choc Bomb… This had to become a book.

John Townsend and his youngest son Christopher Townsend (top left), with his friends Sam and Rob Budd, early 1980s.

name or somehow related to a brand was considered, collected and in many cases catalogued. And this never, ever stopped.

John moved north in 1959 and started a family. He worked as a rep for Birds Eye, covering an area from south Manchester to north Birmingham. He would often return home from business trips with boxes full of packets of gum that he'd bought or traded in the shops he'd visited, which he would pass to his children to sort. The procedure went as follows: first, the children had to unwrap the gum, flatten the wrappers and separate the gum from the cards. The flattened wrappers were filed, the cards stacked and the gum placed in several top-shelf biscuit tins to be carefully rationed. Large A0-sized boards were set up around the house, each marked with large gridded squares on which the card sets were gradually arranged. As soon as a set was complete, it would be taken down, wrapped in the relevant wrapper and filed.

Throughout the 1960s and 1970s, when petrol stations often ran promotional campaigns that involved collecting badges, glasses, flags or football stickers, John would fill up the car and then send his children in to ask the cashier for more tokens or stickers than they were entitled to. Their cheek often worked. And while out and about with his family, John would take any opportunity to stop the car outside a junk shop or antiques emporium, completely disregarding anyone else's needs or schedule. Off he would go, on the hunt for more things.

As far as the house was concerned, collecting seemed just to fit in with the way the family lived. The collection was always there, always expanding, but never taking over the living spaces. However, once the children grew up and left home, their empty rooms were adopted as places to establish new collections or for filing.

John retired in 1984 and became a researcher and archivist for brands including Unilever. In the late 1990s, when the internet gave him 24-hour access to auction sites and forums, his collecting really exploded. Every day for the rest of his life he'd be buying so much that the Post Office organised a van to deliver the mass of incoming envelopes and parcels twice a week. He also started a collecting group known as the MICE Club (Modern Information Collectors Exchange), spreading the idea of collecting contemporary ephemera and knowledge for future generations.

Robin allowed me to take the files and folders back home to document them. I then returned twice more to root around and pick up a couple of additional boxes of material. Over these visits I learned a lot more about the man who had amassed everything.

John Townsend was born in Sutton, Surrey, in 1937. He was orphaned at an early age and spent his childhood in a children's home in Woking. It was here that he started to collect cardboard milk-bottle tops, because he'd noticed they were different every day.

By the 1950s his collecting interests had moved into cigarette silks and he rose to become a leading light in the cartophilic scene (cartophilia being the collecting of cigarette cards and related ephemera). But his passions knew no bounds. His early obsession with cigar and cigarette material soon spilled over into areas unexplored and undocumented – anything with a brand

The MICE Club motto was 'collecting seriously just for fun', a phrase that nails the motivation underlying the John Townsend collection. Money and financial value were never considered – it was all about the objects and all about the future.

In addition to his relentless internet activity, John would also be out most days in Manchester on the hunt for more material. He'd roam the town with his shopping trolley, looking for flyers, recipe cards, phone cards, free postcards, new newspapers – anything printed now for the future. And he'd come back with a trolley load.

By the time of his death in 2014, aged 77, John Townsend had amassed an extraordinary amount of material – some of it catalogued, some unexplored, much of it beyond belief. When I started to dig around in just a small visible fraction of it, I asked Robin how on earth his father had gathered such a mass of extraordinary things while also having a job and three children. Robin simply replied that his father never washed up. Every spare minute he had was spent collecting.

It was clear to me that once John had moved away from the slightly stuffy cartophilia scene, he had developed a specific focus on packaging that came with an item to collect or trade or that featured a special offer. So any 'collect four packet tops and send off to the address below' packaging (fashionable throughout the 1970s) was voraciously sought and he'd even write to the companies concerned to ensure he'd get the promised item or full set, or to secure any missing offer so his collection would be complete. A major tactic was to write to companies that had just closed special offers to ask if they had any surplus items. This often worked. Also, if he spotted special-offer packaging early in its run, John would buy all the relevant packets or items that very day because he knew they could disappear as suddenly as they'd arrived.

If something had been missed in a set or series, he would try to find a picture or make a photocopy simply to document that the missing object had existed. This would remain filed until the actual object was found.

Once he had delved into a new collecting scene or genre, John would explore it intensely, finding out about manufacturers, writing to them for material, stats and facts about what, when and how many they made of something, then often visiting them too. On one of my trips to the house Robin showed me a file of seaside-rock labels. This folder contained hundreds and hundreds of labels that at first all looked exactly the same but on closer inspection were all different, with slightly varying views of Blackpool Tower on each. Also in the file were A4 sheets with the addresses of all the seaside-rock manufacturers, bus timetables and routes showing how John had visited them all in order, to get all their labels. (If it were just up to me, I would have made a book about the mass of seaside-rock labels, but anyway…)

Another method of collecting simply involved asking – friends, friends of friends, colleagues, shopkeepers he met while repping. John would ask everyone if they had any old wrappers, packets, cards… anything. He'd even ask people visiting the house – if, say, a schoolfriend of Robin's was eating a lolly, John would ask if he could have the wrapper. As a result of this relentless asking, family members, neighbours, colleagues and all sorts of other folk would turn up on the doorstep with bags of stuff for John to sort. This explains the varied condition of the items in the collection as well as the boxes and bags full of boxes and bags of incongruous items awaiting John's attention and eventual filing.

Visitors might also get a glimpse of John's amazing collection and collecting brain. If as part of a conversation he heard a relevant trigger or connection, he would spring into action. An example might be a conversation about someone's daughter being in the Girl Guides. On hearing this, John would shoot upstairs and bring down a set of cigarette cards about the history of the Girl Guides – and he'd know all about the origins of the set, its issue numbers and more. His knowledge and expertise led to small features in collecting magazines, books and newspapers and even a show at the Manchester Free Trade Hall.

And always John would see his collection as a social, historical necessity and an important resource, now and for the future.

Well, this is the future for John. And a very small corner of his collection now makes up *Wrappers Delight*.

It has been a three-year process to produce the book – lots of travel, research, photography and heaps of scanning. Decisions about what to include were based on three parameters set by FUEL and myself: 1) we had to like the item for nostalgic reasons; 2) we had to like it for graphic reasons; 3) we had to have room for it in a 240-page book, which was looking problematic as we started with well over 1,500 items I had selected.

So what you have here is the final cut. I've supplied a little information where it was available, but researching some of the rarer brands was very hard indeed. Some seem just to have disappeared. In other cases, where a bit of history could be found, the stories were often sad – mergers, private-equity interventions and buy-outs had left a trail of closed businesses and empty or demolished factories. The book incidentally captures a time when it seemed that large communities across the UK were involved in making imaginative sweets, drinks and snacks. Today, you can whittle that business down to a handful of giants, though it's good to see that companies like Swizzels, which began in 1928 and is just down the road from John Townsend's former home, are still going strong.

In collating and indexing the imagery, we employed John Townsend's alphabetical system, so everything is arranged by brand or manufacturer, not product name. For instance, Double Agents are not under 'D' but are under 'T' for Trebor. John used this filing system consistently as it is the simplest way to find anything.

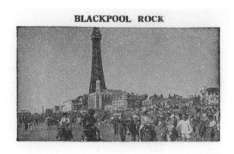

BLACKPOOL ROCK

BLACKPOOL ROCK

BLACKPOOL ROCK

Please also note that *Wrappers Delight* does not claim to be a complete collection of anything but rather is a rare and fabulous mass of gum, drinks, cool confectionery, lollies and weird old memories in one totally delicious book.

I know John Townsend is no longer here, but his very sweet vision of keeping little things for the future to see, enjoy and remember has ended up like this, and I'd like to think he'd be delighted.

IVOR NOVELLO

Legendary entrepreneurial British gum company in operation from 1949 to 1974. The name was created using the initials of the founders: Simon Anysz, Rudy Braun, Douglas and Tony Coakley. The firm began trading in London, eventually moving to Romford, Essex, after expansion. They started producing football cards in 1958, and in 1959 partnered with the American company Topps (makers of Bazooka) to produce some of their US-style gum/card sets. Over the next decade they produced an incredible run of bubble gum and card packages. In 1974, legal wranglings with Topps came to a head and following a long court case A & B C was shut down.

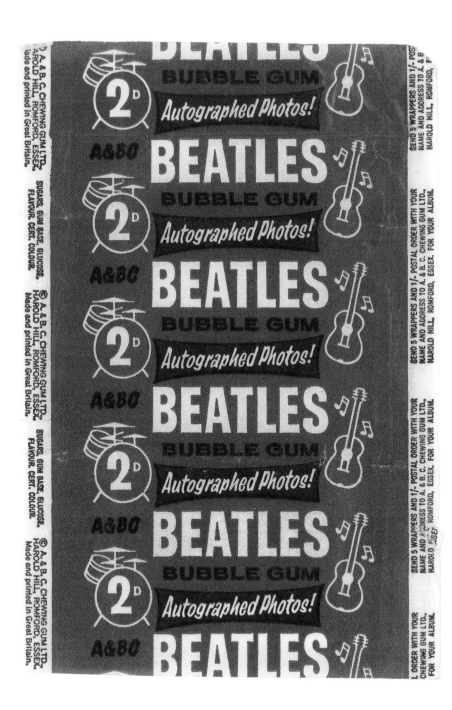

YOO-HOO.... ICE CREAM MAN !

MARY, WE'RE OUT OF TOILET PAPER AGAIN

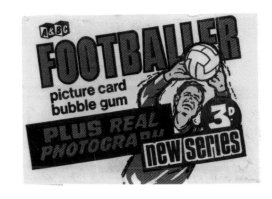

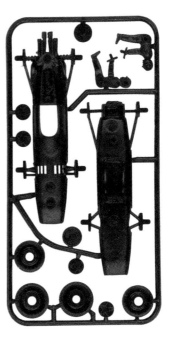

Volvo 164 · Triumph 1300 · Rover three thousand five · Renault 4 · Ford Capri 1600 GTXLR · Volkswagen 1500 Beetle

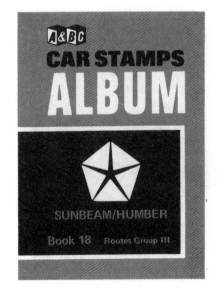

A&BC CAR STAMPS ALBUM

SUNBEAM/HUMBER

Book 18   Rootes Group III

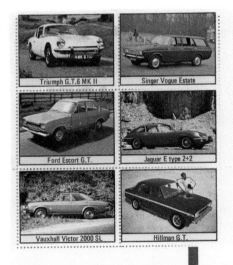

Triumph G.T.6 MK II · Singer Vogue Estate · Ford Escort G.T. · Jaguar E type 2+2 · Vauxhall Victor 2000 SL · Hillman G.T.

M.G. 1300 MK II

Aston Martin DB6 MK II

Hillman Hunter

Rover 3·5 litre Coupé

Volvo 1800 E

Mini Clubman Estate

Munich-based international trading-card manufacturer with subjects ranging from vintage cars to wildlife, TV tie-ins, football and beyond.

Innovative gum company from Illinois. They developed the first sugar-free gum and specialised in desirable novelty packaging. Still trading, now part of Wrigley's.

Brentford-based shandy maker, still going strong, now located in Malaysia.

Formed by Macintosh in 1939, this Halifax-based manufacturer of UK/US gum and inventive gum-card sets was one of the first companies to issue trading-card sets, under the name of 'Thriller Gum'. It became Anglo Confectionery in 1960 and closed in 1986.

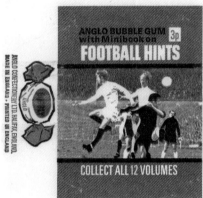

GIANT PICTURE OFFER
For the complete picture (24" x 17¼")
send 10 of these wrappers and a 2/6 or
12½p postal order with your name and
address to :—
Anglo Confectionery Ltd.,
Dept. U, Stoney Royd,
Halifax, Yorks.
MADE IN ENGLAND   PRINTED IN ENGLAND

Reverse side of set of 64 cards
makes giant jig-saw picture.

GIANT PICTURE OFFER
For the complete picture (24" x 17¼")
send 10 of these wrappers and a 2/6 or
12½p postal order with your name and
address to :—
Anglo Confectionery Ltd.,
Dept. U, Stoney Royd,
Halifax, Yorks.
MADE IN ENGLAND   PRINTED IN ENGLAND

Reverse side of set of 64 cards
makes giant jig-saw picture.

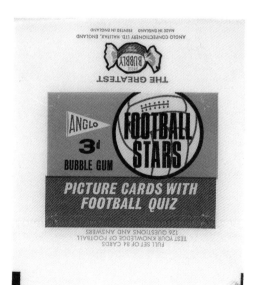

APT (also known as Independent Marketing Services)
were a small Worcester-based drinks company.

ARO is Makro's own-label brand. The cash-and-carry giant that opened its first UK store in Eccles, Manchester in 1971.

A. G. Barr, the Scottish soft-drinks manufacturer, was established in 1875 by Robert Barr. In 1901 they began to produce Irn-Bru, which remains Scotland's top-selling drink.

Founded in Shoreditch, East London, in 1848 by George Barratt, in 1906 it was the largest manufacturer of confectionery in the world. By 1950 the range had expanded across the entire sweet counter, from penny chews to foam shrimps and sweet cigarettes. The company was acquired by Cadbury in 1989 and sold to Tangerine Confectionery in 2008.

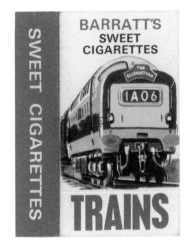

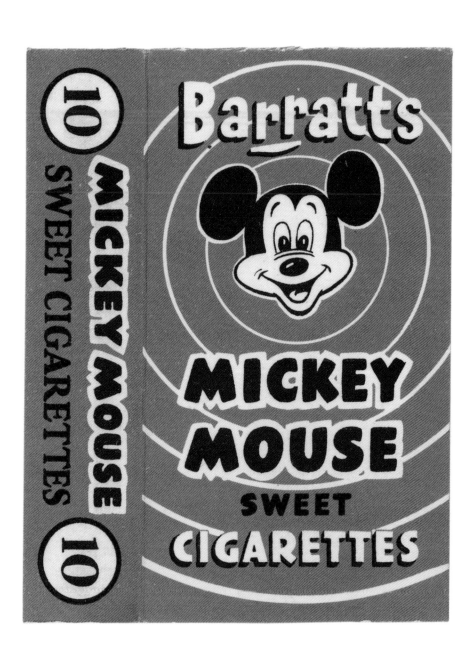

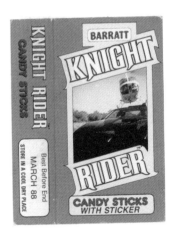

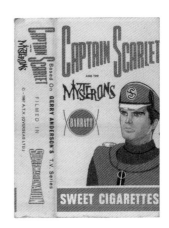

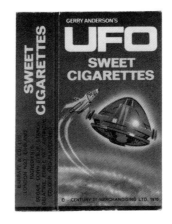

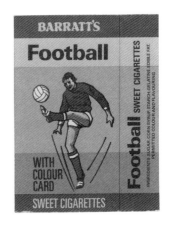

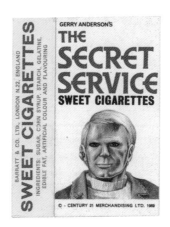

Founded in 1842 by George Bassett, a Sheffield confectioner, lozenge maker and wine trader. In 1899 a Bassett salesman dropped a tray of samples, accidentally mixing up the different sweets. The client was intrigued by the idea of selling 'all sorts' of sweets together, and Liquorice Allsorts were born. In 1989 the company was acquired by Cadbury-Schweppes.

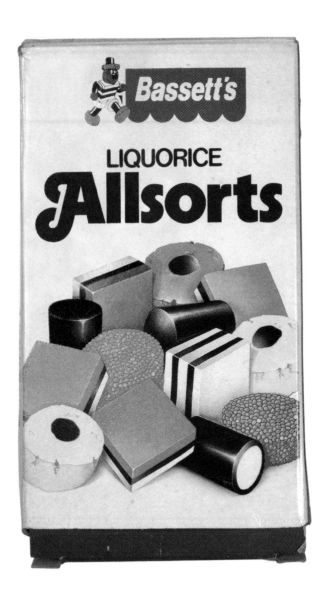

The company was established by chemist Thomas Beecham, who opened his first shop in Wigan in 1847. Over the next century, Beechams built up brands and acquired companies across both the soft-drink and pharmacy sectors. The drinks brands were sold to Britvic in 1986.

This Huddersfield bottler and manufacturer, founded in 1871, supported the temperance movement. In 1959 they were the first company in Europe to can soft drinks and in the 1980s they held 3% of the market. Over-expansion in the early 1990s saw the family lose control of the business and it was finally sold in 1994.

Little is known about this late-1960s confectioner based in Chesterfield.

Founded by Clarence Birdseye in 1923. He developed patents for freezing food, specially fish and the rest is international history. The company employed John Townsend through the 1970s and 1980s. Working as a rep, John made use of various marketing items, including this Fish Finger notepad!

62   R. D. Blackwood & Son

Incorporated in 1947, Blackwood sold their rock on the beach at Blackpool for more than 45 years. Still active today, the company supplies labelled rock for many other people and places.

BLACKPOOL ROCK

Blackwood's of Blackpool

The Old Original Bakewell Pudding Shop

Ingredients: Sugar, glucose syrup, flavouring and
colours E102, E142, E110, E123, E127, E132, E122.
R. D. Blackwood (Prod.) Ltd. Post Code FY4 4NE

BLACKPOOL ROCK

Ingredients: Sugar, glucose syrup, flavouring and
colours E102, E142, E110, E123, E127, E132, E122
R. D. Blackwood (Prod.) Ltd., Blackpool FY4 4NE

BLACKPOOL ROCK

Ingredients: Sugar, glucose syrup, flavouring and colours
E102, E142, E110, E123, E127, E132, E122, E124.
R.D. BLACKWOOD (Prod.) LTD., Blackpool FY4 4NE

SALTCOATS ROCK

Ingredients: Sugar, glucose syrup, flavouring and
colours E102, E142, E110, E123, E127, E132, E122.
R. D. Blackwood (Prod.) Ltd. Post Code FY4 4NE

CONWAY CENTRE ROCK

Ingredients: Sugar, glucose syrup, flavouring and
colours E102 E110 E122 E123 E124 E127 E132 E142
R. D. Blackwood (Prod.) Ltd. Post Code FY4 4NE

BLACKPOOL ROCK

Ingredients: Sugar, glucose syrup, flavouring and colours
E102, E142, E110, E123, E127, E132, E122, E124.
R.D. BLACKWOOD (Prod.) LTD., Blackpool FY4 4NE

SOUTHPORT ROCK

Ingredients: Sugar, glucose syrup, flavouring and
colours E102, E142, E110, E123, E127, E132, E122.
R. D. Blackwood (Prod.) Ltd. Post Code FY4 4NE

'NARDINI' – LARGS

Ingredients: Sugar, glucose syrup, flavouring and
colours E102, E142, E110, E123, E127, E132, E122.
R. D. Blackwood (Prod.) Ltd. Post Code FY4 4NE

YORK ROCK

Ingredients: Sugar, glucose syrup, flavouring and colours
E102, E142, E110, E123, E127, E132, E122, E124.
R.D. BLACKWOOD (Prod.) LTD., Post Code FY4 4NE

THE MENAI CENTRE
LLANFAIRPWLLGWYNGYLLGOGERYCHWYRND-
ROBWLLLLANTYSILIOGOGOGOCH

Ingredients: Sugar, glucose syrup, flavouring and
colours E102, E142, E110, E123, E127, E132, E122.
R. D. Blackwood (Prod.) Ltd. Post Code FY4 4NE

PAIGNTON ROCK

Ingredients: Sugar, glucose syrup, flavouring and
colours E102, E142, E110, E123, E127, E132, E122.
R. D. Blackwood (Prod.) Ltd. Post Code FY4 4NE

JENOLAN CAVES

MINARET, RIVER CAVE
LETTERED ROCK
CANDY
Ingredients: SUGAR,
GLUCOSE SYRUP,
ARTIFICIAL FLAVOUR
& COLOUR
Net 50g
Made in England by
R. D. Blackwood Ltd.
BLACKPOOL
For Souvenir Rock Dist.
P.O. Box 306   Albury
© **D. DRURY** 1970   7

BLACKPOOL PLEASURE BEACH ROCK

Ingredients: Sugar, glucose syrup, flavouring and colours E102, E142, E110, E123, E127, E132, E122.
R. D. Blackwood (Prod.) Ltd., Blackpool FY4 4NE

BRIGHTON ROCK

Ingredients: Sugar, glucose syrup, flavouring & colours E100, E102, E110,
E122, E123, E124, E127, E131, 133, E142, E150, E151, E153, 155, E171
CATTLIN, BRIGHTON

MANCHESTER CITY
FOOTBALL CLUB LTD.
Founded 1894
European Cup Winners Cup 1970
First Division League Champions
1937 1968
Runners-up: 1904 1921
Second Division
League Champions
1899 1903 1910 1928 1947 1966
Runners-up: 1896 1951
F.A. Cup Winners
1904 1934 1956 1969
Finalists: 1926 1933 1955
Football League Cup Winners 1970
Finalists: 1974
F.A. Charity Shield Winners
1937 1968 1972
Finalists: 1934 1956 1969 1973
Made by
R. D. BLACKWOOD LTD.
BLACKPOOL
© Football League

MULL OF KINTYRE ROCK

Golden Casket (Greenock) Ltd
Ingred: Sugar, glucose, permitted colours & flavouring

CLEETHORPES ROCK

Ingredients: Sugar, glucose syrup, flavouring and colours
E102, E142, E110, E123, E127, E132, E124,
R.D. BLACKWOOD (Prod.) LTD., Post Code FY4 4NE

LETTERED
ROCK CANDY

Ingredients: SUGAR,
GLUCOSE SYRUP,
ARTIFICIAL FLAVOUR
& COLOUR
Net 50g
Made in England by
R. D. Blackwood
Ltd.
BLACKPOOL

For Souvenir Rock Dist. P.O. Box 306 Albury   © D. DRURY 1970 126

THANK YOU FOR SHOPPING COLES

Sugar Confectionery
LETTERED ROCK
CANDY

50 gms

Made in England by
R. D. Blackwood Ltd
BLACKPOOL
For Souvenir Rock Distbrs.
P.O. Box 306   Albury
© D. DRURY 1970 30

ROCK WITH THE BEATLES

Rock–Ingredients: Sugar, Glucose, Permitted Colours & Flavourings
Manufactured by R. D. Blackwood Ltd. Post Code FY4 4NE

Strange UK drinks brand based in Middlesex during the
mid-1970s. Full company name was PGMA Bob Ltd.

Established in 1840, this Scottish starch manufacturer patented cornflower in 1854. Eventually they moved into custards and by 1962 were producing Knorr soups.

66   Brooke Bond

Founded in Lancashire in 1845, the tea-trading company is famous for its Red Label and PG Tips brands and, of course, the collectable cards that were included in every box from 1954 onwards. It is now part of Unilever.

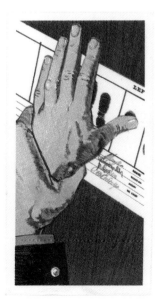

An inventive biscuit, cake and crisp company, the Burton bakery started in the mid-1800s and Burton's Biscuits was established in 1935. Wagon Wheels rolled out in 1948 and Jammy Dodgers launched in 1960.

Established in Birmingham in 1824 by a wealthy Quaker, John Cadbury. The best-selling Dairy Milk Chocolate was introduced in 1905. The company merged with J.S. Fry and Sons in 1919. Flake, Creme Eggs and Crunchie were introduced in 1920, 1923 and 1929 respectively. The rest is history, and of course, a small village called Bournville.

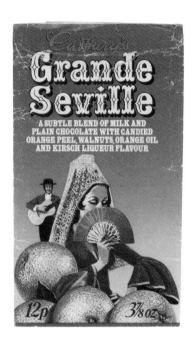

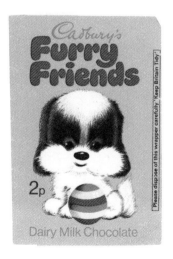

STRIKERS

Strikers go right to the heart of the battle. They need courage, strength and boldness to go for goals without waiting. Plenty of shooting practice is never wasted. Try marking targets about 3 feet in diameter on a wall, between 10 and 20 yards distance away. Also practice volleys and half-volleys by shooting first time at crosses and passes from the wings.

Cadbury Limited, Bournville, Birmingham

Please dispose of this wrapper carefully 'Keep Britain Tidy'

SOCCER TIP No.5 STRIKERS

Cadbury's **Soccerbar** Dairy Milk Chocolate

Guaranteed by Cadbury

Cadbury's **Roobarb**

Cadbury Limited, Bournville, Birmingham

Dairy Milk Chocolate

When Roobarb called the tune

One morning Roobarb gets a HUGE parcel. "It's my do-it-yourself Bagpipe kit" he tells Custard, and hurries off to glue it all together.
Just then a parcel arrives for Custard! It's a do-it-yourself VIOLIN kit – free to every next-door-neighbour of someone who buys the Bagpipe kit!
"What a wonderful fiddle," says Custard.

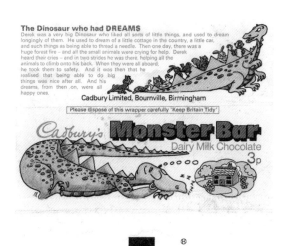

The Dinosaur who had DREAMS

Derek was a very big Dinosaur who liked all sorts of little things, and used to dream longingly of them. He used to dream of a little cottage in the country, a little car, and such things as being able to thread a needle. Then one day, there was a huge forest fire – and all the small animals were crying for help. Derek heard their cries – and in two strides he was there, helping all the animals to climb onto his back. When they were all aboard, he took them to safety. And it was then that he realised that being able to do big things was nice after all. And his dreams, from then on, were all happy ones.

Cadbury Limited, Bournville, Birmingham

Please dispose of this wrapper carefully 'Keep Britain Tidy'

Cadbury's **Monster Bar** Dairy Milk Chocolate   3p

The 'Immovable-Coin' Trick
Glue a coin to the pavement. People will try and pick it up without success.

Cadbury Limited, Bournville, Birmingham

Please dispose of this wrapper carefully 'Keep Britain Tidy'

Cadbury's **LAUGHS** Dairy Milk Chocolate   3p

No.2 laugh on the back

72008 Þ

 HOW TO GET YOUR curlywurly FLASHERS

To obtain your free card of ten Curlywurly Flasher badges simply collect any six Curlywurly wrappers and send them together with a 2½p stamped addressed envelope to:
CURLYWURLY FLASHERS · P.O. BOX 203 · CANTERBURY · KENT

Cadbury's **curlywurly** 3p FREE Flashers *see back for details*

CARAMEL COVERED   IN MILK CHOCOLATE

TEAR HERE

Slough-based sweet-cigarette and card manufacturer, heavily into TV-based products.

Dating from the late-1960s, this may be the same company as Big Chief (page 59). They were based in Chesterfield and mainly produced fun bags.

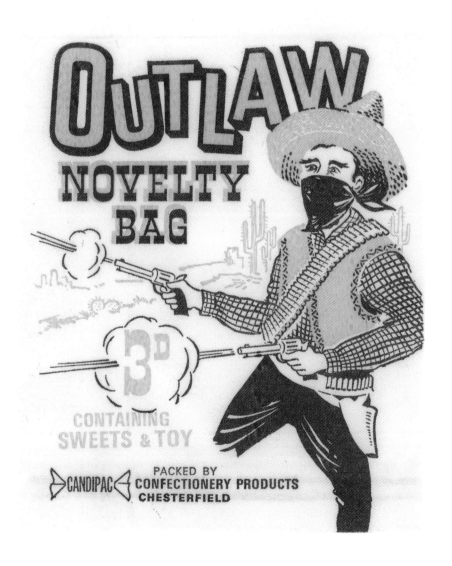

A gum, tattoo transfer and novelty manufacturer based
in Milan.

Founded in New Jersey in 1912, in the late-1960s they invented and introduced the Blow Pop, the first lolly with a bubble gum centre.

A bubble gum and trading-card manufacturer from Slough, the company was established in the mid-1950s and continued until the mid-1970s.

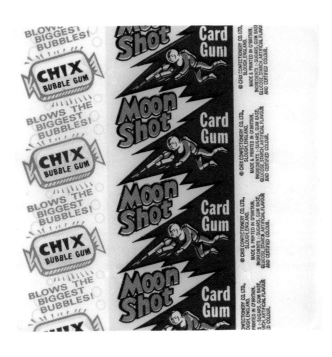

An early UK manufacturer of sweets, fun bags and
sweet cigarettes, founded in the late-1950s and based
in Blackpool. They even started their own hobby club
for keen sweet-eaters.

Short-lived sweet-cigarette and sport-card manufacturer from the early 1960s, based in Slough.

A London-based manufacturer of gum and trading cards in the 1960s. Collect ten 'Zak Stamps' from Destination Moon (overleaf) and you could send off for a large Astronaut poster.

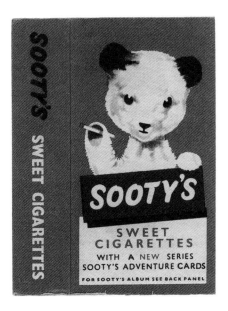

Como Confectionery and Gaycon (a production and licensing company) were based at the same address in London's Regent Street during the 1950s and 1960s.

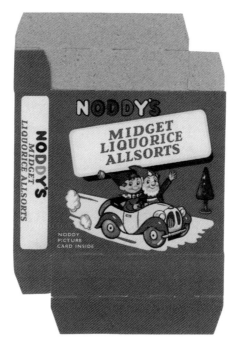

In the 1970s, Consort Drinks were produced by Independent Food Service, a small grocery company from Harrow.

This popular soft drink, originally produced by Thomas Evans Ltd, in South Wales, was bought by Beecham in 1958. The 1960s and 1970s saw memorable advertising campaigns such as the 'Corona Fizzical'. Corona lorries distributed bottles weekly door to door. The brand stopped trading in 1990.

A   FREE   BADGE   WITH   EACH   BOTTLE

A very large privately owned Danish gum producer, founded in 1915. The Dandy name first appeared in 1939. Throughout the 1950s and 1960s the brand expanded hugely through new products (such as Stimorol), clever marketing and simple eye-catching ideas. They sold their gum brands to Cadbury Schweppes in 2002.

S 68

S 98

C 30

S 30

S 1

T 28   PRINTED IN DENMARK

T 18   PRINTED IN DENMARK

N 79   Printed in Denmark

T 70   PRINTED IN DENMARK

N 1   Printed in Denmark

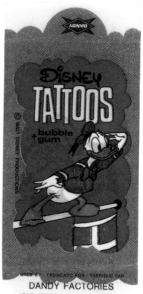

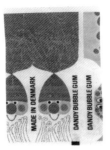

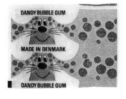

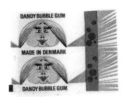

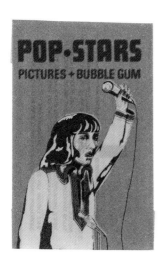
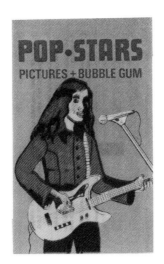

A sweet-cigarette maker, based in Farnham, Surrey, between 1960 and 1962. Which is odd, because I grew up there and never heard of them.

Dunkin

Busy Spanish maker of gum, rub-on tattoos and more.

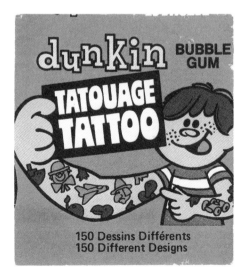

T 77   PRINTED IN DENMARK

T 8   PRINTED IN DENMARK

T 73   PRINTED IN DENMARK

T 27   PRINTED IN DENMARK

T 23   PRINTED IN DENMARK

T 98   PRINTED IN DENMARK

T 3   PRINTED IN DENMARK

T 84   PRINTED IN DENMARK

T 83   PRINTED IN DENMARK

The Egg Marketing Board was established by the British Government in 1956 to stabilise the market following a period of falling sales. Lively advertising campaigns (by Ogilvy & Mather) included 'Go to work on an egg' and 'E for B' (egg for breakfast). The Board was closed in 1971.

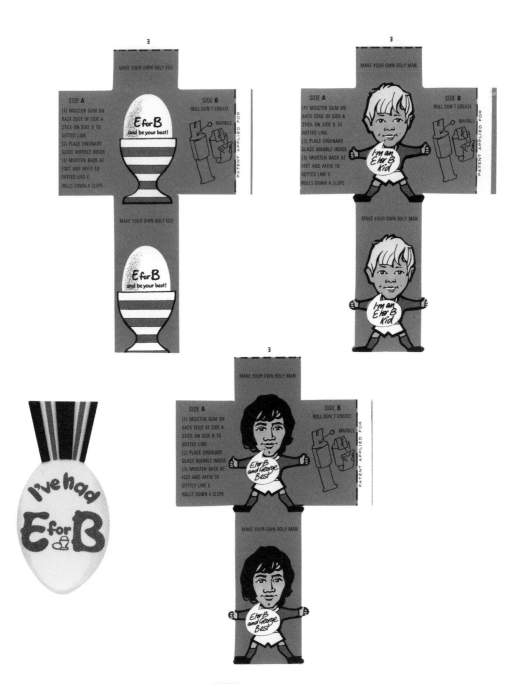

The petrol and oil giant, Standard Oil of New Jersey, ran this football club badge offer – a free badge with every four gallons of petrol – between 1971 and 1972.

Based on Kilburn High Road, London, FKS were a prolific and popular producer of football stickers from 1966 onwards. They were declared bankrupt in 1987.

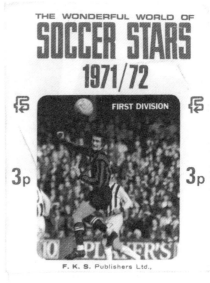

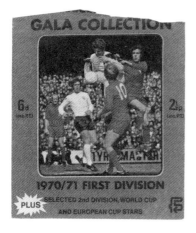

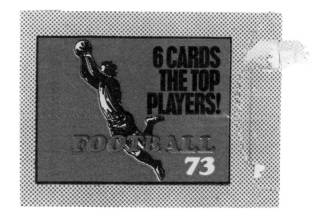

Philadelphia's Fleer Corporation, founded in 1885, were the first company to manufacture bubble gum successfully and began to produce trading cards in 1923. They were declared bankrupt in 2005.

J.S. Fry & Sons were founded in Bristol in 1822. They created the first filled chocolate sweet in 1853 and launched Turkish Delight in 1914. The company merged with Cadbury in 1919.

Sweet maker Thomas Fryer opened his Victory Works factory in Nelson, Lancashire, in 1890. One of his employees created a mould for jelly bears, but the results looked more like little humans. Initially known as 'unclaimed babies', you can work the rest out yourself. They also manufactured bubblegum and Victory Vs.

SPACE INVASION

BALLOON RACE

COWBOYS AND INDIANS

AIR BATTLE

Alien Space Ship. The Robots attack!

Venus. A timely departure.

A peculiar gum manufacturer based in Barcelona. This bizarre Identikit is the only item from the brand in the John Townsend collection.

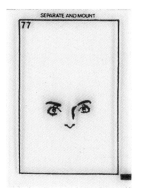

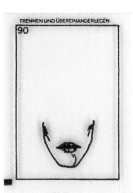

A drinks company founded by George Barraclough in Yorkshire, c.1830, producing table waters and lemonade. It went funky in the 1960s with Geebee pop.

Glenville, established in 1970, were based in Greenwich, London. According to their trademark application, the company produced 'Fruit flavoured preparations in liquid form, for use in making frozen confections in the nature of water ices'.

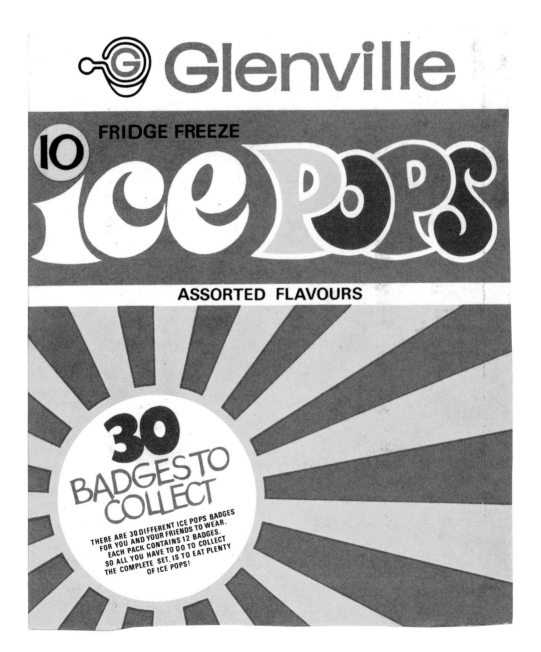

A little-known company from Morley, West Yorkshire.

Founded in Edinburgh in 1947, the company was named after a potato variety. Still operating, it is now owned by Tayto (Northern Ireland) Ltd.

Made by Arthur Holland of Southport, a legendary toffee and chew producer. By 1961, the company had become the biggest toffee manufacturer in the world. Based in Bristol and Southport, it later diversified into other confectionery, including sweet cigarettes and chews. Chewitts (originally called Chewzits) were created in 1963.

  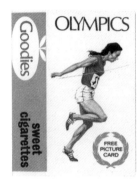

 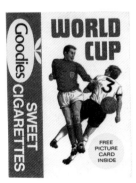

Obscure manufacturer of frozen lollies and ice cream
during the 1970s.

Hendry's of Scotland, mineral-drink manufacturer,
established 1906, closed 1973.

The Camden-based drinks producer, established in 1873, was named after its owner, Thomas Idris. He had changed his surname from Williams, having fallen in love with Cader Idris, a Welsh mountain. The company was bought by Britvic in 1987.

The French chocolatier was established in 1914 in Troyes by the wife of a biscuit maker. The company expanded rapidly after World War II, and is now a global high-end chocolate brand.

Established in the 1760s, this Dundee company was once the largest sweet manufacturer in the UK. The factory closed in 1990.

Oddly, this appears to have been manufactured by Littlewoods, the Liverpool-based football pools and retail giant.

Knight Foods from Nottingham produced drinks for a brief period during the 1970s.

'Kenyan Produce', based in Slough. Established in 1853, this major British snack manufacturer became part of United Biscuits in 1968. It is now owned by Intersnack, Germany.

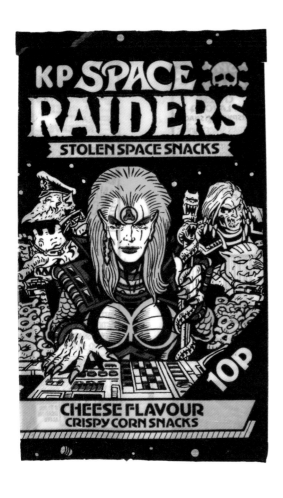

Dublin-based Space Dust manufacturer. 'Pour into your mouth and enjoy the popping, tingling and crackling sensation on your tongue!' A playground favourite from the early 1980s.

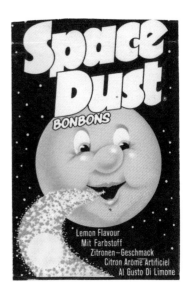

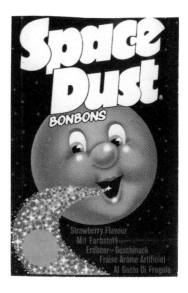

Obscure 1960s Japanese sweet manufacturer.

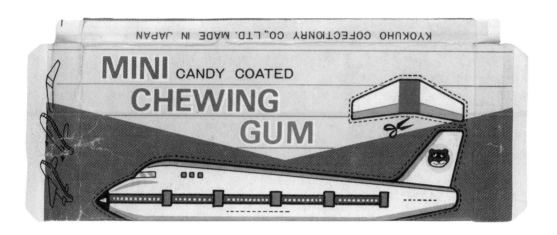

Founded by Sol Leaf in Chicago in 1940, the company made various gums and trading cards, eventually expanding into Europe. In the 1990s, Leaf became one of the world's top-ten confectionery companies. It was especially strong in non-chocolate products such as pastilles and chewing gum.

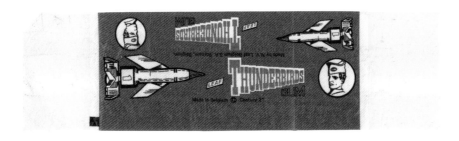

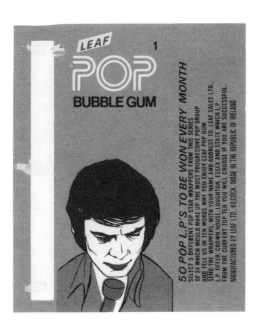

Die Haut anfeuchten, das Bild andrücken und abziehen.
© DC Comics Inc.1982

LEAF SUPER HEROS
Mouillez legerement la peau, appuyez le tatouage
et retirez le papier protecteur.
Lightly moisten skin, press on tattoo and peel off.
De huid bevochtigen, op tatoeëring drukken en aftrekken.

LEAF SUPER HEROS
Mouillez la peau, appuyez le tatouage et retirez
le papier protecteur.
Wet skin, press on tattoo and peel off.
De huid bevochtigen, op tatoeëring drukken en aftrekken.
Die Haut anfeuchten, das Bild andrücken und abziehen.
© National Periodical Publication Inc. 1975

Die Haut anfeuchten, das Bild andrücken und abziehen.
© DC Comics Inc.1982

LEAF SUPER HEROS
Mouillez legerement la peau, appuyez le tatouage
et retirez le papier protecteur.
Lightly moisten skin, press on tattoo and peel off.
De huid bevochtigen, op tatoeëring drukken en aftrekken.

Die Haut anfeuchten, das Bild andrücken und abziehen.
© DC Comics Inc.1982

LEAF SUPER HEROS
Mouillez legerement la peau, appuyez le tatouage
et retirez le papier protecteur.
Lightly moisten skin, press on tattoo and peel off.
De huid bevochtigen, op tatoeëring drukken en aftrekken.

…d bevochtigen, op tatoeëring drukken en aftrekken.
Die Haut anfeuchten, das Bild andrücken und abziehen.
© DC Comics Inc.1982

LEAF SUPER HEROS
Mouillez la peau, appuyez le tatouage et retirez
le papier protecteur.
Wet skin, press on tattoo and peel off.

LEAF SUPER HEROS
Mouillez la peau, appuyez le tatouage et retirez
le papier protecteur.
Wet skin, press on tattoo and peel off.
De huid bevochtigen, op tatoeëring drukken en aftrekken.
Die Haut anfeuchten, das Bild andrücken und abziehen.
© National Periodical Publication Inc. 1975

Founded in London in 1959, Letraset produced innovative graphic tools, such as rub-down lettering. Action transfers for kids started in 1964. I had some. Letraset is now part of Winsor & Newton.

PRINTED IN ENGLAND BY LETRASET GK161

Longley's

In 1886 the Manfredi family began selling ices from carts. In 1967 they opened a factory in Warrington, making the famous Teddy Bear. Today the company still thrives.

A small Leeds-based ice-cream maker from the mid-1960s (nothing to do with the successful Longley Farm dairy of today).

A confectionery works founded in the late-1800s in Glamorgan, Wales. It is now owned by the Turkish Ulker group.

A small and short-lived Margate- and London-based manufacturer of chocolate cigarettes.

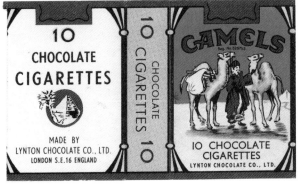

East London sweet-cigarette importer and distributor, whose chocolate cigarettes were named and packaged very much like real cigarettes.

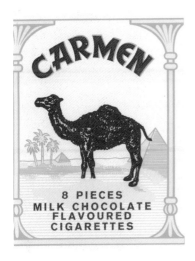

An ice-cream brand established in 1924 as an offshoot of J. Lyons and Co. During the late-1960s and 1970s it was a prolific producer of film and TV tie-in lollies. The company was sold to Nestlé in 1992.

Mac Fisheries was originally a fishmonger founded by William Lever (one half of Lever Brothers), after World War I. It later morphed into a supermarket chain, Mac Food Centres, whose own-brand products included soft drinks. The company was sold in 1979.

The Scottish biscuit makers McVitie & Price were founded in 1830. Their Chocolate Digestive was introduced in 1925 and the Jaffa Cake in 1927. Today they are the best-selling biscuit maker in the UK, with an average of 52 chocolate digestives being eaten every second in Britain..

Manufactured by The Moffat Group, a wholesale and drink-production company based in Woodford, Essex and operating through the 1970s.

A Dutch trading-card producer, based in Leiden. The company was founded after World War II and named after Field Marshall Montgomery. Their prolific output included pop, football, TV culture and more.

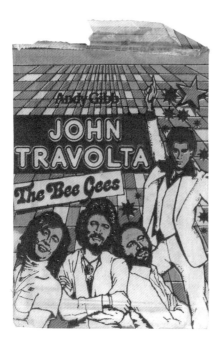

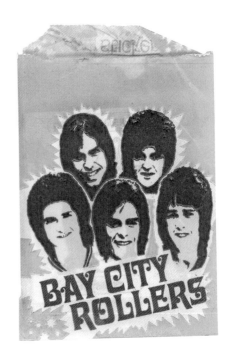

Bristol-based lolly manufacturer. Seems to have melted away into the past.

National

National Benzole was a petrol brand sold in the UK from 1919 until the late-1960s.

Formula One Racing Car
2⅞ ins. 55–1 scale.
Matchbox Superfast. Free from your National Dealer

The Swiss-based multinational, founded in 1860, is the
largest food company in the world, a chocolate monster.

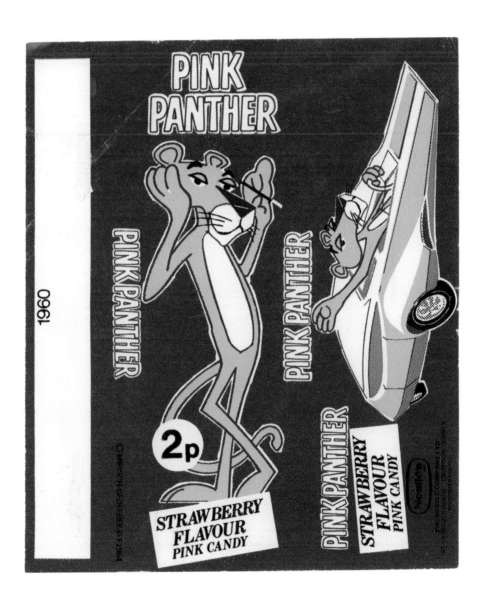

Established in the 1970s, this hugely popular soft-drink brand was manufactured by the Dorset brewery, Hall & Woodhouse, established in the 18th century.

The massive international trading-card manufacturer, founded in Modena, Italy, in 1961. Fifteen million packets of stickers were sold in 1961. Early in the 1970s, they were the first company to introduce self-adhesive stickers.

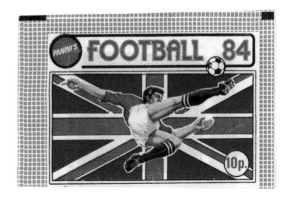

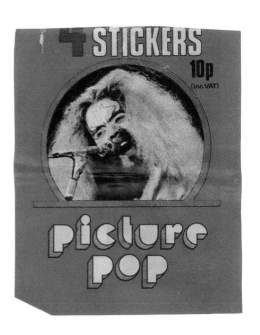

Founded in Warrington, Cheshire, in 1844, Albert Peacock's Penny Bazaar eventually grew into a large supermarket chain and clothing brand.

Incorporated in 1953, this confectionary company was based in Newark, Nottinghamshire. Their Sugar Pigs were apparently very popular.

Pendleton & Sons

A family-run lolly business from Liverpool. Established in 1935, it was sold to Lyons Maid in 1988.

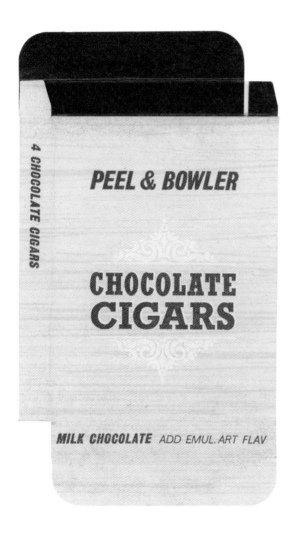

This Slough-based sweet, sweet-cigarette and card manufacturer had good international distribution and was very active throughout the late 1950s, 1960s and early 1970s. Their prolific output left behind a large array of collectable TV and comic-related card sets as well as some superb packaging. Early licensing was key to their success, using contemporary icons such as Popeye and Superman to bewitching effect.

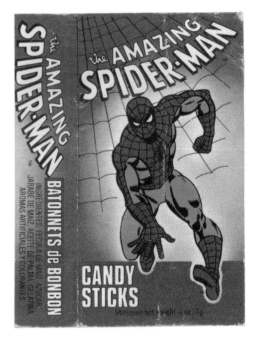

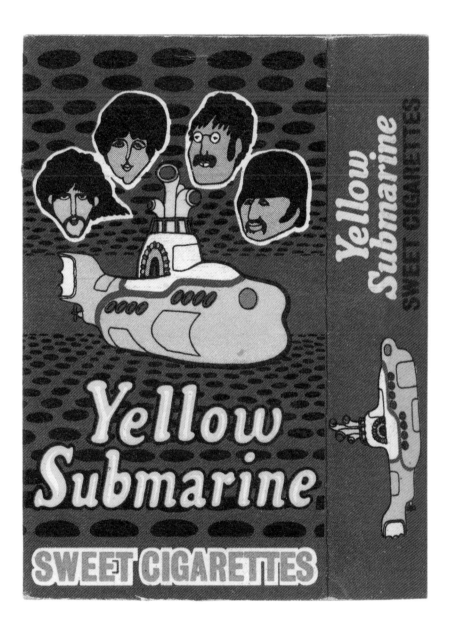

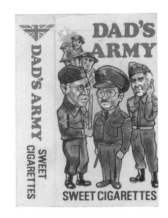

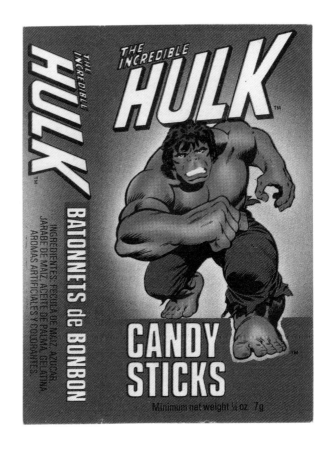

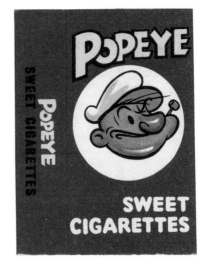

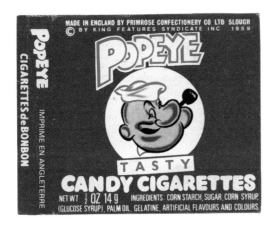

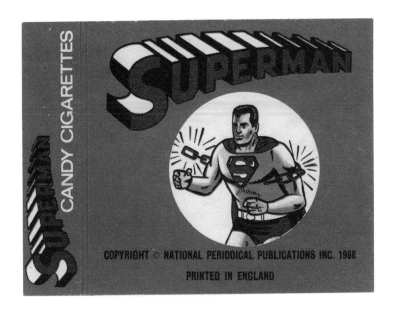

The famous lemonade was first produced by Robert and Matthew White in Camberwell, London, in 1845. The comapny was taken over by Whitbread in the 1960s and later sold to Britvic. The song for the popular 1973 'Secret Lemonade Drinker' advertising campaign was written by Ross McManus, with backing vocal by his son, Declan, aka Elvis Costello.

Founded in York in 1862, the company introduced many incredibly popular confections, including: Black Magic (1934), Aero (1935), Kit Kat (1935), Smarties (1938), Yorkie and Lion Bars (1976).

Part of Standard Brands, the company was based in their 1950s modernist Aintree factory outside Liverpool.

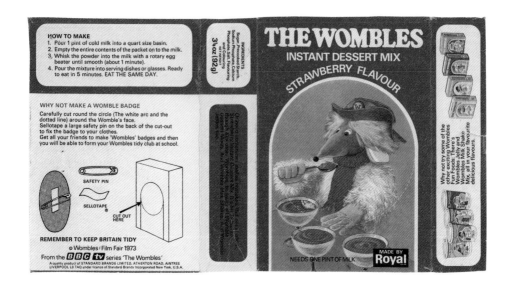

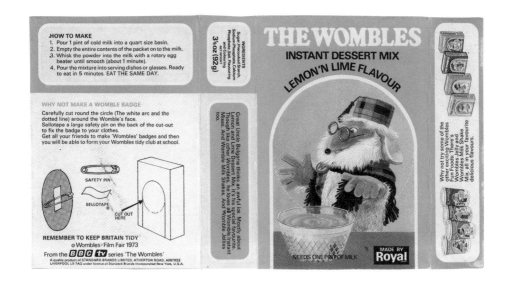

The 150-year-old supermarket chain established an in-house design studio to develop a range of pioneering own-label packaging throughout the 1960s and 1970s.

The Swiss beverage brand, founded in 1783, merged with Cadbury in 1969 to become Cadbury Schweppes. In the years that followed, the company bought a number of other large brands and is now itself part of Mondelez International.

Based in Maidstone, this toffee manufacturer was founded by Sir Edward Sharp in 1911. The company was later bought by Trebor, who continued to produce sweets in Maidstone until 1991.

A family-owned drinks manufacturer from Folkestone, founded in 1886. Silver Spring products were very popular throughout Kent, especially Bing, a unique soft drink. In the 1970s they created the Rola Cola and Spring-Up brands. Following a change of ownership in 2009 the company was finally liquidated in 2013.

Founded in Cricklewood in 1920 by Frank Smith and friends. Known for their crisps, the company also produced a range of Big D Peanuts (D for Dallas, the origin of the nuts), which enjoyed successful pub marketing throughout the 1970s with the patented 'Babe Board' – a scantily clad woman obscured by packets of peanuts. As each bag was sold, more of the woman would be revealed. Smiths is now owned by PepsiCo.

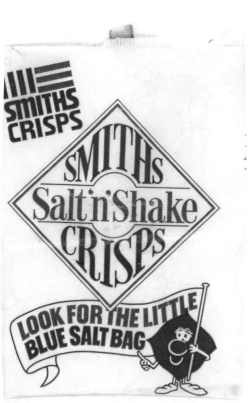

An important early Dutch manufacturer of small sweets, chews, gum and cards. Packaging ranged from movie stars to scenes of outer space.

Soccer Pops

This short run of football-based pop drinks featured some of the most famous players of the time. They were manufactured by ISMA London in the late-1960s.

This super-cool and innovative 1960s card, sweet and novelty company was based in London. They were the first to license James Bond, The Saint and Thunderbirds imagery for gum trading cards, even progressing to film stills and transparencies. In addition, they occasionally used creations from the Fleetway Publications' roster.

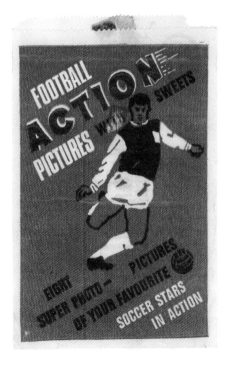

No. 55 TIN-TIN (A MALAYAN NAME MEANING 'SWEET') DAUGHTER OF KYRANO. © A.P. FILMS LTD ISSUED BY SOMPORTEX LONDON A SERIES OF 72 PICTURES.

No. 26 EARTH DRILLING 'MOLE' TRANSPORTED IN THUNDERBIRD 2 – POD 2. © A.P. FILMS LTD ISSUED BY SOMPORTEX LONDON A SERIES OF 72 PICTURES.

No. 42 AQUA-NAUT GORDON TRACY CO-PILOT OF THUNDERBIRD 2 AND DRIVER OF THUNDERBIRD 4. © A.P. FILMS LTD ISSUED BY SOMPORTEX LONDON A SERIES OF 72 PICTURES.

Licensed by A. P. FILMS (Merchandising)
Ltd. England

Send 24 wrappers to THUNDERBIRD 2,
30 St. John's Lane, London E.C.I. with
stamped self-addressed envelope for your
FREE THUNDERBIRD KEY RING. Your
envelopes must be stamped. Offer applies
to U.K. only.

INGREDIENTS:
sugar, gum base, softeners, artificial flavours,
starch and U.S. certified colours.

Made in Holland by
MONTY FACTORIES
for SOMPORTEX LTD. London E.C.I.

73 PICTURES
IN COLOUR
FROM THE
T.V. SERIES

THUNDERBIRDS

BUBBLE GUM

© 1966 A. P. FILMS LTD.

46

THUNDERBIRDS

THUNDERBIRD 1

NIGHT LIFE
The swinging Lady Penelope
fronts a small beat group at one
of London's most exclusive night
clubs. With her wonderful voice,
she is a smash-hit with the
audience, but she is really on
duty.

© 1966 A. P. Films Ltd.
A SERIES OF 73 PICTURES
issued by Somportex Ltd. London E.C. 1

The Dutch multinational chain store, established 1932.

Henry Faulder & Co. was an inventive grocer and confectioner founded in Stockport in 1893. Renamed the Squirrel Chocolate & Confectionery Company in 1930, their factory was acquired by Cadbury in 1936, later becoming Squirrel Horn. Squirrel sweets are now manufactured by Tangerine Confectioners in Dorset.

This late-1960s drinks manufacturer was based in London's South Moulton Street.

A range of drinks produced throughout the 1970s and 1980s by Benjamin Shaw & Sons of Huddersfield. Water from the Pennines was sometimes used in the manufacturing process.

This Allied Bakeries brand of sliced white bread is now
part of the Associated British Foods empire.

A short-lived late-1970s sparkling drinks company.

In the 1950s this small Manchester-based producer of sweet cigarettes manufactured trading cards on the subject of transport.

Swizzels

A Derbyshire confectionery manufacturer, established in 1928 and still going strong! Not really surprising when your products include Love Hearts and Drumsticks.

This long-established Liverpool factory has been making sweets since the 1930s. It is now owned by a company based in Blackpool.

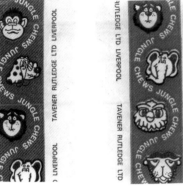

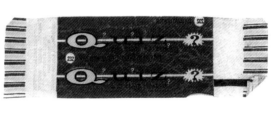

The famous Glasgow brewery dates back to 1740. The 'Lager Lovelies' began in the late 1950s when it was decided to add images of women to the cans under the heading 'Housewives' Choice', followed by a recipe using lager as an ingredient. The 1960s saw the production of cans featuring local girls. By the end of the 1980s this 'booze and birds' combination was viewed as old-fashioned and subsequently shelved.

The company was founded as Tonis in 1937 by Italian-born Toni Pignatelli. Ice-cream vans took to the street in 1951 and the business later expanded into parlours and ice-cream manufacturing.

Founded in New York in 1938, the company name shown their intention to be 'tops' in their field. In 1950 they began packaging trading cards with gum to great effect. Their Bazooka bubble gum was first produced after World War II and in 1953 the hugely popular comic-strip character 'Bazooka Joe' was introduced on its wrappers.

0-530-0-8

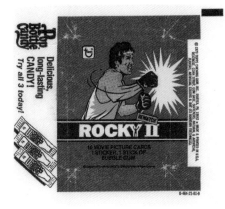

ALL NEW SERIES

SUPERMAN™
THE MOVIE™

MANUFACTURED IN REP. OF IRELAND
BY TOPPS IRELAND LTD., CORK
FOR DISTRIBUTION IN U.K. AND EIRE
BY TREBOR LTD., MAIDSTONE.

WITH
1 STICK
BUBBLE GUM

TM AND © DC COMICS INC 1978

A confectionery company established in 1907 and based in Forest Gate, East London. Trebor is Robert, the name of one of the founders, spelt backwards.

('La la la la la') *Look-in* was the teen TV magazine based around pop music and ITV television programmes. Published every Thursday, it ran from 1971 to 1994.

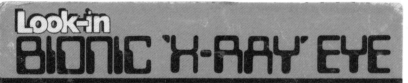

Look-in
BIONIC 'X-RAY' EYE

TO ENSURE TOP PERFORMANCE: hold the card close against one eye and shut the other. View through the 'eye's' small aperture. Hold your hand (or foot, or other bony object to be viewed), at  arm's length away from you and spread your fingers. Always view against quite bright light such as a window etc., (NOT directly into the sun), preferably from a slightly darker position.

Presented with Look-in, Junior TVTimes, Oct.1976.

This famous tea brand began in Birmingham in 1903. The name is derived from the Chinese word for 'doctor'. The company started bagging tea in 1967. This set of Doctor Who tea cards dates from 1976 and stars Tom Baker as the fourth incarnation of the Doctor. Typhoo is now owned by one of India's oldest conglomerates.

Village was probably an own-label brand for the (now defunct) Alliance chain of supermarkets.

Under the influence of the temperance movement, this
soft drink was invented in Manchester in 1908 as a
health tonic. It is still manufactured today.

The snack manufacturer was established in Leicester
in 1948. The company produces 11-million packets of
crisps a day at the world's largest crisp factory.

The origins of the business can be traced to 1786 when Richard Wall opened a butcher's stall in London. Every summer demand for meat fell so early in the 20th century, to compensate for this drop in sales, Wall's conceived the idea of making ice cream. The company is now owned by Unilever.

Wall's
SEA SIDE SAUCY

"WHERE'S MY SANDWICH –
I MUST HAVE LEFT IT BEHIND"

STRAWBERRY FLAVOUR ICE CREAM
(CONTAINS NON-MILK FAT),
STRAWBERRY FLAVOUR JELLY CENTRE,
WITH SUGAR BALLS.

Wall's RED ARROW

STRAWBERRY &
VANILLA FLAVOUR
ICE LOLLY

NEW   Wall's
Warlord

THE ACTION
LOLLY

CHOCOLATE AND MINT
FLAVOUR ICED LOLLY

Wall's
DALEK'S DEATH RAY

CHOCOLATE AND MINT
FLAVOUR ICED LOLLY

Wall's   NEW
STAR·SHIP
2000
ICE LOLLY

FREE WITH THIS LOLLY
STAR ALARM
ASK THE SHOPKEEPER

LEMONADE, RASPBERRY
& MIXED FRUIT
FLAVOUR STAGES

Wall's
SKY RAY

PLANE SPOTTER
GUIDE · SEE BACK

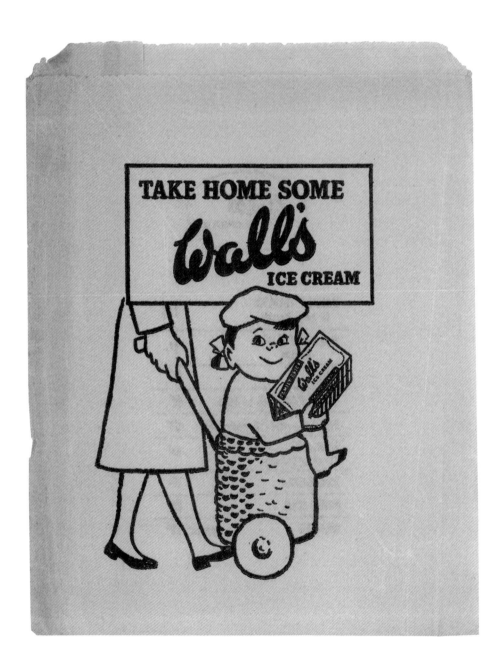

This North Shields confectioner produced sweets such as caramel bonbons, sherbets and lollies. In 2004, dwindling sales lead to the factory closing.

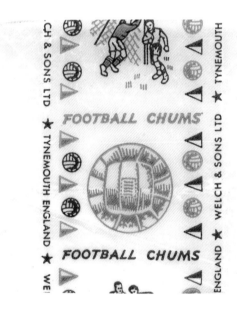

Winfield was Woolworths' own-label brand from 1963 to 1983. Unfortunately it was never considered to be as good quality as branded equivalents.

The famous American chewing-gum company established in Chicago in 1891. It is now the largest manufacturer of chewing gum in the world.

Keep your
country tidy!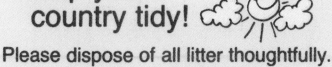

Please dispose of all litter thoughtfully.

MADE IN ENGLAND BY THE WRIGLEY COMPANY LTD., PLYMOUTH

Thank you to the following people who backed this book:

Aaron Rice
A C F Wilson
Adam
Adam Green
Adam Humphries
Adam McLean
Adam Mussett
Adam Selby
Adam Wheway
Ade Fleury-Holland
Adrian Pike
Adrian Self
Adrian Smith
Adrian Zak
Al Murphy
Alan Beeson
Alan Bentley
Alan Duncan
Alan McKinnon
Alasdair Corrigall
Alex Jennings
Alex Moresby
Alex Rudolph
Alex-ish Petridis
Alfonso Ambles
Ali Munro
Alis Templeton
Alisdair Wood
Alistair Fitchett
Alister Babb
Allan Roberts
Allison Jung
Al Napp
Ambrose Chapel
Andreas Stiller
Andrew Begg
Andrew Bromelow
Andrew Caws
Andrew Collingridge
Andrew Collins
Andrew Cook
Andrew Fisher
Andrew Green
Andrew Hale
Andrew Hall
Andrew Nicholas
Andrew Perks
Andrew Preshous
Andrew Rutland
Andy Aldridge
Andy Holloway
Andy Jarvis
Andy Knott
Andy Lee
Andy Lowe
Anita Gray Saito
Anne Ward
Anthony Goldstraw
Anthony Iamurri
Anthony Jarrett
Anthony Tripi
Anthony Whiting
B Yates
Backer Name
Barry Ashworth
Barry Fellows
Barry Sowle
Ben Dakin
Ben Javens

Ben Jeffreys
Ben Johnson
Ben Norland
Ben Read
Ben Richardson
Ben Scott
Benjamin Tisdall
Benn Peacock
Bill Brewster
Blair Hurm Cowan
Bob Fischer
Bob Jaroc
Brent Quigley
Bryony
C Hathway
Cameron Lindo
Camilla Deakin
Carl Seebode
Caroline Alexander
Caroline Champion
Carolyn & Steve Castle
Cath Lane
Catherine Mackay
Chap
Charles Anthony Goddard
Charlotte Benton-Hughes
Cheetah Breaks
Chris
Chris Allen
Chris Bauer
Chris Cameron
Chris Carter
Chris Cobbs
Chris Crites
Chris Lane
Chris Matthews
Chris Phillips
Chris Purdon
Chris Warren
Chris Wood
Christian Homersley
Christopher Brosnahan
Christopher Houston
Clare Kelly
Clay Gardner
Clive Thirlwall
Colin Price
Colours May Vary
Connie C
Conny Fanta Lundgren
Craig Brackenridge
D S Reifferscheid
Daddybones45
Daiji Shikama
Daisy Robinson
Dale Everett
Damon
Dan Adams
Dan Edwards
Dan London
Dan Tombs
Dan Williams
Danny
Danny Kelly
Darren Edwards

Darren Giddings
Darren Lewis
Darren Manion
Darren Stephens
Dave B
Dave Clayton
Dave High
Dave Mitchell
David Allen
David Barraclough
David Boulter
David Clayforth
David Gibson
David Godfrey
David Goodge
David Grover
David Grover
David Hasler
David Lawson
David Leister
David Luff
David Masters
David Mellor
David Nulty
David Osman
David Plaice
David Tatlow
David Tinkham
David Yapp
Dead Ringers Shop
Dean Vipond
Debby Viles
Denis O'Brien
Derek Collie
Derek Ham
Derek Mantle
Derek Roden
Diceindustries
Dickon Ross
Dom Romeo
Douglas Candano
Dwayne Bell
Eamonn Griffin
Eamonn Murphy
Ed Owen
Edmund Slater
Edward Bewick
Elaine Cassell
Emily Reese
Eric Fennessey
Eric Horstman
Eric Lagendijk
Evan Skeithe
EvilPRGuy
Flinch25
Francis Robinson
Franklin
Fraser Bensted
Fred Deakin
G W Lang
G Circosta
Gareth Bellamy
Gareth Bramley
Gareth Halfacree
Gareth Lonnen
Gareth Moses
Gareth Richards
Gareth Wild
Gary

Gary Fowles
Gary Grimmer
Gary James
Gary Northfield
Gary Shirley
Gary Tomkins
Gary Woodward
Gavin Sutherland
Gemma & Isra
Gentlearwig
Geoffrey Dolman
Georgie
Gita Malhotra
Glen Rollings
Glen West
Glenn Armstrong
Glenn Law
Glyn Roberts
Graeme Ward
Graham Clark
Graham Lovatt
Graham Noble
Graham Olek
Graham Tomlinson
Grant Debnam
Greg
Greg Marshall
Gregory Pritchard
Hannah
Hannah Lawrence
Hannah Simpson
Harvey Williams
Hazel Ireland
Hector Cruz
Helen Birkett
Helen Skinner
Henning Stuenitz
Herr Dokta
Hesham Sabry
Howard Griffiths
Hugh Leoidsson
Iain
Iain Gray
Iamjamesward
Ian
Ian Bailey
Ian Green
Ian Jeremy Shirley
Ian Johnsen
Ian MacMillan
Ian McIlroy
Ian Moore
Ian Morris
Ian Pakes
Ian Pile
Ian Quann
Ian Robertson
Ian Shelley
Ian Warner
Ian Yorke
Jack
Jack Driscoll
Jacob W Fleming
Jake
Jake Morrison
James Clark
James Cox
James Dawes
James Endeacott

James Harley
James Hollingworth
James Hyman
James Kontargyris
James McNally
James Newport
James Watson
James Wright
Jamie Baverstock
Jan Singleton
Jane Harper-Otner
Jared Taylor
Jason Domers
Jason Draper
Jason Garrattley
Jason Heeley
Jason Jackson
Jason Liebig
Jason Smith
Jay Eales
Jay Espindola
Jd Michaels
Jean-Paul Sparkes
Jeff Barrett
Jeff Doherty
Jeff Stoneking
Jeffrey C Devey
Jeremy
Jeremy Brown
Jeremy Dye
Jeremy Holmes
Jeremy Rathbone
Jess Price
Jessica
Jessica Jones
Jim Jupp
Jim K Davies
Jim Millington
Jodie Lowther
Jodie Wood
Joe Chatham
Joe Coleman
Joe McIntyre
Joel Proudfoot
Joel Zimmerman
John Broadley
John Clarke
John Duckworth
John Farrelly
John Gleaves
John Jervis
John Miyasato
John Moulson
John Power Jr
John V Keogh
Johnny Horth
Jolyon Shotton
Jon
Jon Hobbs
Jon Shore
Jonathan
Jonathan Beech
Jonathan Carr
Jonathan Elliman
Jonathan Jones
Jonathan Kelly
Jonathan Knowles
Jonathan Sharp
Jonnie Siese